A Note to Parents and Teachers

DK READ⁓⁓ S is a co⁓⁓ling r⁓ading programme for childr⁓⁓ ⁓ ⁓ ⁓ ⁓ ⁓ ⁓ ⁓ designe⁓ ⁓ ⁓ conjunction w⁓ leading literacy experts, including Cliff Moon M.Ed., who has spent many years as a teacher and teacher educator specializing in reading. Cliff Moon has written more than 160 books for children and teachers. He is series editor to Collins Big Cat.

Beautiful illustrations and superb full-colour photographs combine with engaging, easy-to-read stories to offer a fresh approach to each subject in the series. Each DK READER is guaranteed to capture a child's interest while developing his or her reading skills, general knowledge, and love of reading.

The five levels of DK READERS are aimed at different reading abilities, enabling you to choose the books that are exactly right for your child:

Pre-level 1: Learning to read
Level 1: Beginning to read
Level 2: Beginning to read alone
Level 3: Reading alone
Level 4: Proficient readers

D0415221

The "normal" age at which a child begins to read can be anywhere from three to eight years old. Adult participation through the lower levels is very helpful for providing encouragement, discussing storylines and sounding out unfamiliar words.

No matter which level you select, you can be sure that you are helping your child learn to read, then read to learn!

LONDON, NEW YORK, MUNICH,
MELBOURNE, AND DELHI

Series Editor Deborah Lock
Art Editor Mary Sandberg
Managing Art Editor Rachael Foster
Production Editor Sean Daly
Production Claire Pearson
Picture Researcher Harriet Mills
Jacket Designer Natalie Godwin

Reading Consultant
Cliff Moon, M.Ed.

Published in Great Britain by
Dorling Kindersley Limited
80 Strand, London WC2R ORL

Copyright © 2009 Dorling Kindersley Limited
A Penguin Company

2 4 6 8 10 9 7 5 3
DD504 - 12/08

A CIP catalogue record for this book
is available from the British Library

ISBN: 978-1-40533-859-2

Colour reproduction by Colourscan, Singapore
Printed and bound in China by L. Rex Printing Co. Ltd.

The publisher would like to thank the following for their kind
permission to reproduce their photographs:
(Key: a=above; b=below/bottom; c=centre; l=left; r=right; t=top)

Alamy Images: John Angerson 28b; Paul Collis 8-9 (main image);
Danita Delimont 9tr, 12-13, 25tr, 32tl; Franck Fotos 31cr; JTB Photo
Communications, Inc/Haga Library 16-17; Tom Mackie 26-27; Jeff
Morgan alternative technology 23tr; Photofusion Picture Library 3c;
The Photolibrary Wales 10-11, 11tr, 32cla; Robert Harding Picture
Library Ltd 13tr; Henry Westheim Photography 14, 15tr. **Corbis:**
Jean Pierre Amet/Sygma 30; Bob Krist 20-21 (main image); Benedict
Luxmoore/Arcaid 29; Getty Images: Jeremy Horner/Riser 17t;
Photonica/Franco Zecchin 7bl, 32clb; Stuart Westmorland/Stone 24-25.
Imagestate: Goran Burenhult 18cl, 32cl. **naturepl.com:** Eric Baccega 6,
7, 35br; Constantinos Petrinos 18-19 (main image), 19tr. **Robert Estall
Photo Library:** Carol Beckwith & Angela Fisher 22 (main image).
Shutterstock: Clouston 21br, 32bl; Dana E. Fry 5; Andy Z. 4.
Still Pictures: K. Hennig 27

Jacket images: *Front:* **Photolibrary:** Franck Guiziou.
Back: **Shutterstock:** Clouston tr. **naturepl.com:** Eric Baccega tl.

All other images © Dorling Kindersley
For further information see: www.dkimages.com

Discover more at
www.dk.com

Contents

 READERS

Homes
Around the World

Written by Max Moore

A Dorling Kindersley Book

Most of us live in houses or flats.

They are usually made of bricks
or concrete.

But not all homes in the world
are like this.
Some people live in unusual
homes.

Would you like to live high above the ground?
Some people in forests and jungles build treehouses.

They use bamboo, vines and wood from the forest to make their homes.

treehouse

Suppose you went outside,
dug up some clay and
then built a house with it.
People in very hot places
can do this.

The sun dries
the clay into strong
adobe bricks.

adobe

These cone-shaped, mud-brick homes are called beehive houses. Their tall, cone-shaped roofs help to keep them cool inside.

All the hot air
rises to the top
of the house.

beehive house

What would it be like to live
on a lake?
Some people build their homes
on floating islands made of reeds.

They add a layer of fresh reeds
every few months.

reeds

Some fishermen build
wooden houses on stilts
over the water.
People walk along walkways
to get to shops, work and school.

walkway

Houses on stilts are also sometimes built on land. People walk up a ramp to get into their homes. Cows, pigs, horses and chickens are kept under their houses.

stilts

ramp

Would you like a house shaped
like a boat?
These wooden houses are
called tongkonans.
They are the homes of
the Toraja people.

tongkonan

Some houses have many carvings
of plants and animals inside.

Have you ever moved to
a new house?
Some people move several times
every year.

They can fold up their houses and set them up again somewhere else. These houses are covered with animal skins.

yurt

Straw tents can be moved, too. Straw is a light material but it is also strong and warm and doesn't let water in.

Straw can also be used to make the walls of homes that don't move.

Suppose you lived in a cold place. Some people used blocks of snow to build igloos, which they lived in during the winter.

These igloos kept out the wind and were warm inside.

In hot places, some people live in houses carved into rocks. These homes are warm in the winter and cool in the summer.

Some people build houses
in ways that help the planet.

This house is heated only by
the sun.

This house is made from
old shipping containers.

These houses use less energy
and material than most homes.

Some people build houses just for fun.
These homes are made to look like a mound of bubbles and an alien spaceship.

In the future, people may build their homes in other unusual ways.

Glossary

Adobe
a material made from dried earth and straw

Beehive house
a cone-shaped, mud-brick house

Tongkonan
a wooden house shaped like a boat

Treehouse
a house built high up in the trees

Yurt
a round home that can be moved around